Walks

Around The

New Forest National Park

4th Edition

by

Members of the New Forest Group of the
Ramblers' Association
www.newforestramblers.org.uk

Printed by The Minster Press Wimborne Dorset BH21 1JQ
© New Forest Group, Ramblers' Association April 2000
Re-walked and substantially updated, Autumn 2011

FOREWORD

We hope you find this book of walks useful, and pleasant to read. The New Forest has been around for about 1000 years and we very much enjoy walking in it, so we want to share it with you. In 2005 it gained National Park status, sadly on much narrower boundaries than those originally designated by the Countryside Agency after very thorough consultation with all parties, including The Ramblers. However, within its boundary now set out by Government, the National Park Authority has the duties of "conserving and enhancing natural beauty, wildlife and cultural heritage" and "promoting opportunities for understanding and enjoyment of the area's special qualities by the public". If they succeed in both these purposes, we expect that our grandchildren's grandchildren, and their descendants will still be walking with joy in the Forest in 1000 years to come.

To the casual visitor, the woodlands and wide heathlands of the Forest may seem to be unchanging, but the reality is quite different. Change has been massive in the past and continues apace today. Even over the last few years large tracts of coniferous and mixed woodland have been cleared at the behest of conservationists, who wish to see them converted back into heathland. River channels have been made to meander again, and bogs have been recreated and extended. Despite the tranquillity of its ancient woodland glades and open heaths, the Forest has been a place of controversy since it began as a recreation area for foreign conquerors - Canute and William I. Most people know that William II, who spoke Norman French, not English, was mysteriously shot and killed in the Forest. Not so many know that where he died was most probably where we take you on Walk 15, rather than at Rufus Stone. Did you know that Alice Lisle, the last woman to be beheaded in England, had a house in the Forest? See Walk 4, Page 19. We have taken great care in updating our walking instructions to take account of many recent changes. A page of "Forest Walking Advice" at the beginning of the book, and the maps and notes with each walk, give you all the basic information you need to enjoy a Forest walk. Each walk description includes "Points of Special Interest" to help you enjoy their beauty and understand some of the history, both ancient and modern. We like to think that this is the most reliable and interesting book of walks in the Forest, so if you do find any errors, please let us know via our website.

Last but not least, a word of thanks to all the walk originators after whom each walk is named, to the officers of the Forestry Commission and others who re-walked and checked all the walks, and to the many other helpers whose names appear in the Acknowledgements at the end of the book.

Enjoy your walking,

John Thackray (New Forest Group, The Ramblers)

YOUR CHOICE OF WALKS

See walk location map inside front cover
Times include 1 hour for stops and are based on 4km/hr = 2 ½ miles/hr walking speed.

Walk Names & Locations	No.	Page	Distance	Hours
Chris & John - East of Fordingbridge	1A	7	8km (5m)	3
Chris & John - East of Fordingbridge	1B	10	5km (3m)	2¼
Molly & Geoff - Bramshaw	2	12	10km (6m)	3½
Roy - Fritham	3	15	13km (8m)	4¼
Derek & Marie - North of Ringwood	4	19	6½km (4m)	2½
Alan & Margaret - West of Lyndhurst	5	22	8km (5m)	3
Reg & Hilda - West of Lyndhurst	6	24	8km (5m)	3
Anne - South East of Ashurst	7A	26	8km (5m)	3
Doreen & Tony - South East of Ashurst	7B	28	7km (4½m)	3
Anne & Trevor - West of Hythe	8	31	9km (5½m)	3¼
Vic & Rose - Burley	9	34	6½km (4m)	2½
David & Bernice - West of Sway	10	37	8km (5m)	3
Audrey - Brockenhurst	11	39	9km (5½m)	3¼
Dave & Gill - South of Brockenhurst	12	42	6½km (4m)	2½
Glynis & Frank - South of Fawley	13	44	9km (5½m)	3¼
Ruth - Milford/Keyhaven	14	48	10km (6m)	3½
Audrey - East of Lymington	15	53	10km (6m)	3½

Walk descriptions give directions for finding the car parks and the walk.

FOREST WALKING ADVICE

Walk Length and Time needed is given for each walk. These are based on a normal uninterrupted walking speed of 4 kms/hr or 2½ miles/hr. Kms have been given because 4 kms/hr means that you can walk straight across a 1 km square marked on all Ordnance Survey Maps in 15 minutes, or diagonally across it in 21 minutes. Shorter distances are given in metres. An adult step is about ¾ metre: 4 steps = 3 metres

Direction This is shown as North (N), North East (NE), East (E), SE, S, SW, W, NW. It is best to have a compass, but on a sunny day without one, you will know direction at any time of day. Early in the morning (6-7 am) the sun is broadly E, by Noon it is S and by early evening (5-7 pm) it is broadly W.

Maps It is always best to carry a good map. If you want to stray off our maps or go a different way, we recommend the Ordnance Survey Explorer Map "New Forest" (OL22): orange cover 1:25000 scale. This covers all the walks and shows most detail. Map references (Map Ref.) are given for the car park at the start of each walk. The reference system used is explained on all OS maps.

Equipment and Warnings It is possible to walk in trainers, strong flat shoes or sandals in dry weather, but parts of the Forest can be wet at any time. Especially where wet ground or bogs are mentioned, it is better to wear boots or comfortable wellies. It is always wise to have spare warm and wet weather clothing with you as well as something to drink, and a seasonal hat. Do not leave handbags and valuables, animals or children behind in the car. Even in the boot valuables may not be safe! In the summer there are sometimes ticks on bracken, gorse etc, which could get onto your skin. Almost invisible to start with, they swell and typically the next day they start to itch. You need a tick picker from a vet to get them out safely and afterwards give the spot a dab of antiseptic. If it doesn't calm down after 48 hours, see a doctor as the tick might just be infected with Lyme disease.

KEY

✳	Start and/or finish of walk	■ +	Building and Church
➡	Direction of walk	~⌇~	Stream with bridge and footpath
⇨	Alternative or diversionary route	⪪	Water feature
⑤	Reference point in instructions	ꟼꟼꟼꟼꟼ	Bank or hill
═══	Main road	ʼʼʼ ᵃ ʼʼʼ	Heathland (sometimes marshy)
══	Other roads	+++++++	Railway
═════	Access track to property	♀ ♀	Deciduous trees
‒ ‒ ‒ ‒	Footpath or track	♣ ♣	Coniferous trees
CP	Car Park		

4

Bolderwood Colours - Vic Ruston

Ponies near Whitten Pond - Vic Ruston

Acorn Harvest in Bramshaw Wood
Robin Fletcher CA

Fallow Deer - Vic Ruston

6

CHRIS & JOHN'S WALKS

1A. ASHLEY, GODSHILL AND ANCIENT CASTLES

Walk Length and Time: 8 kms (5 miles) 3 hours
Walks 1A and 1B can be joined together to make a relaxed all day "Figure of 8"
Starting Point: Ashley Walk Car Park, Map Ref: SU186157
Either A338 to Fordingbridge and then NE on B3078 through Godshill past Fighting Cocks PH and Car Park is on right after 1 km (½ mile). **Or** from M27 (Jct 1) go NW on B3079 and B3078 towards Fordingbridge. Car Park on left after 11 kms (7 miles).

Points of Special Interest

This is a beautiful walk through woodland and some open forest. It is mainly dry underfoot in summer. It starts from the ridge of high ground running NE from Godshill, near Fordingbridge, from which there are excellent views over the open forest and into the valleys. Brune's Purlieu at the start of the walk is land taken from the forest and given by the monarch in medieval times for services rendered (such as providing a daughter to warm his bed, some say!) It is interestingly different because here the land has been divided into small fields which are farmed instead of being managed as open heathland for grazing (like Ogden's Purlieu 4 kms due S). Frankenbury, and Castle Hill later on, are fascinating earthworks. Frankenbury is more than 200 metres in diameter. Its name reminds one of the ancient battles of the early Celtic (British) inhabitants with the invading Anglo-Saxons – and presumably Franks - after the Romans left. Unfortunately Frankenbury can only be viewed from the side, but the extensive earth ramparts of Castle Hill can be explored at leisure. They make a good place for a picnic stop. The Castle Hill Viewpoint looks west over the Avon Valley and the battle ground where the West Saxons vanquished the giant King of the Ancient Brits (Nathan Leod) in 519 AD, so changing the course of English history by firmly establishing the Kingdom of Wessex. Godshill Inclosure on the return leg of the walk is an interesting example of an area of woodland originally enclosed to keep ponies and other large animals out. It contains fine specimens of oak, chestnut and beech, as well as douglas fir and other Forestry Commission conifers.

Walking Instructions

✱ From car park cross road *carefully* and head NW downhill with fence line on your left, for approximately 400 metres. *Turn left* through gate heading SW along cart track. Continue through another gate, you are now in Brune's Purlieu.

(1) Just after you come to a thatched cottage on left *turn right* along gravel track.

7

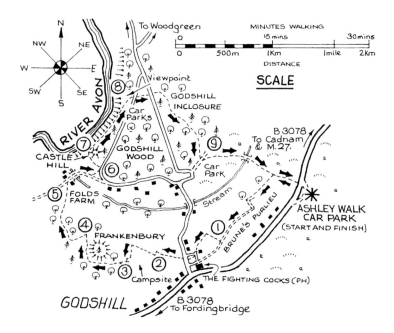

GODSHILL

60 metres before Lane End Farm *turn left* onto footpath next to a double gate where there is a yellow footpath sign. At the end of this sometimes overgrown footpath you come to a rusty old gate which leads out onto the road. (The Fighting Cocks pub is about 200 metres further up this road on the left and you could start and finish the walk there.) Cross road to footpath clearly signposted. This will have taken approximately 30 minutes from start of walk. Climb over stile and walk forward on grassy field path heading NW. Pass horse trough on your left, through gate on left, crossing hedge line and out into field.

(2) Continue in same direction as before for 200 metres, keeping the hedge on your right, to second stile through thick beech hedge. Carry on straight along path between hedges until you come to another stile on the left. (This is just before another stile on the right, so if you come to this second one you will know you have missed the one you need!) Over stile, into field and go straight ahead on edge of field with hedge *on your left*. You actually walk around the campsite at the end of field so it is *right* and then *left*, over stile into lane.

(3) *Turn right* and go past small sewage plant into wood (beech, pine and holly trees) and downhill. Frankenbury Castle Ring is in holly trees on right-hand side of track. Climb bank to have a look, but unfortunately you cannot go in as it is fenced off and private land. Walk on forest path through these woods to NW corner of Frankenbury and go downhill.

(4) *Continue bearing left* (W) and downhill and do not take track on right

8

which heads N. At the bottom you can see a stile ahead on the right going into meadow. Over stile and right, then take the inviting green track heading N parallel with a stream. Go forward to gate and stile. Cross stile onto delightful woodland track still heading N, with stream always on left. Another track joins, but continue ahead onto a gravel track. Bear left and then turn right along the Avon Valley Path.

(5) You are halfway round and should have taken about an hour and three-quarters. Continue past Folds Farm, keeping straight ahead past large greenhouses on your right-hand side. Cross bridge and go over stile or cattle grid onto gravel track by Folds Farmhouse. *Turn left* (NE) on gravel track to join the road to Castle Hill heading **NE.**

(6) *Turn immediately left* after only 20 metres, just past cottage (Armsley) on corner, and take a narrow often overgrown small footpath steeply uphill by signs for fire hydrant and water main. At the top of this path a track joins from right but cross and continue up. House on left has extended its grounds, but when you get to a level bit, *go right,* then *immediately left* again up to very top of hill. The earthworks are the remains of the Castle Hill Ring and Bailey.

(7) Cross ring and carry on NE through several earthworks. (River Avon is steeply downhill on left through trees.) Keep left of tarmac road to Castle Hill Viewpoint and Car Park where there are seats to enjoy view. About two and a quarter hours from start by now, and the last section should take three quarters of an hour.

(8) Go through gate on right between two car parks. Take track straight ahead through holly bushes, 150 metres to road. Cross road through gate into forest again. Take right-hand track (easy to miss this) heading SE. The forest here is a mixture of conifers, beech, oak and chestnut. Another track joins from left but keep straight on up to cross gravel track at 5-way junction, and onto road and car park.

(9) *Turn left* and *swing right* cutting diagonally downhill, heading E to valley bottom and trees at northern end of Brune's Purlieu. Cross stream by bridge and uphill by fence and tree line which is on your right and up to road, cross it back to Ashley Walk Car Park again.

CHRIS & JOHN'S WALKS
1B. PITTS WOOD, WW2 SUBMARINE PENS AND BOMB TARGETS

Walk Length and Time: 5 kms (3 miles) 2¼ hours
Walks 1A and 1B can be joined together to make a relaxed all day "Figure of 8" walk.
Starting Point: Ashley Walk Car Park, Map Ref: SU186157
For directions, see previous walk.

Points of Special Interest
Although this walk starts at the same point as Walk 1A, it has a quite different character. Apart from Lodge Hill and Pitts Wood, open heathland – the home of falcons and other birds of prey – dominates the landscape. The whole of this area, Leaden Hall and much more was taken over in 1940 by the Air Ministry as a bombing and firing range, and then enclosed for top security with a 6 foot high chain link fence, as part of the national war effort. Remains can be found to this day by the observant walker. The 'tumulus' at point (3) on the walk provides a particularly good vantage point. The concrete exposed near the top tells of its history as a dummy submarine pen for bombing practice, and part-filled circular craters show near and not so near misses. Lodge Hill, just before the entrance to Pitts Wood, has ancient oaks which survived the wartime devastation. It makes a fine point for a picnic stop. Beware of boggy ground after prolonged wet weather, through and after Pitts Wood – much recent felling plus some new bogs and heathland. An alternative route back at this point lies northward through Ditchend Bottom along the E bank of Ditchend Brook. Especially on a summer day, you may see cricket at Godshill **(7)** and possibly buy an ice cream from the mobile kiosk.
See also "Ashley Walk, its Bombing Range, Landscape & History" by Parker & Pasmore, New Forest Research & Publication Trust, Hatchet Gate Farm, Hale, Fordingbridge, Hants SP6 2ND.

Walking Instructions (**NB** Pitts Wood Inclosure is no longer fenced.)
✱ Set off in a SE direction from car park, go downhill and into valley using any of the three paths. Cross Ditchend Brook in about 450 metres and take clear gravel track uphill. Halfway up take the pleasant green path running parallel to the track on your left, through Cockley Bushes where you may see Highland cattle and deer. Path rejoins gravel track on Cockley Hill (400 metres) veering in an easterly direction. Carry on across Little Cockley Plain (another 400 metres).
(1)   Take *right* fork in track (SW). Go downhill for 400 metres, veering S to Lodge Hill. (Good shelter and picnic spot. About 30 minutes to this point without stops). Walk on through Lodge Hill heading S and into Pitts Wood Inclosure. Ignore path about 40 metres inside and go straight ahead over bridge over stream in wood

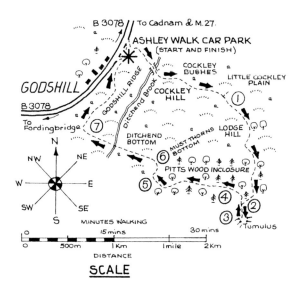

and gently uphill heading S for about 400 metres.

(2) After leaving the Inclosure bear slightly *right* and cross another wide gravel track. Continue S over brow of hill until 'tumulus' with gorse on it appears on your left.

(3) Walk up onto 'tumulus', good view all round. Note concrete in 'tumulus' and partially filled circular bomb craters all around - largest is to SW and is water filled. Retrace your steps for 200 metres and then go back through same gate into Pitts Wood Inclosure heading N.

(4) Take path on *left* in 20 metres heading slightly N of W and follow this through mixed woodland for 1 km (15 minutes). Keep as near straight ahead as you can heading broadly W. Ignore path crossing diagonally in about 400 metres, and then two other paths (which cross after 700 metres and 900 metres).

(5) Turn right (N) at path junction with no path on left to Must Thorns Bottom ditch and ford.

(6) Go through gateway to path outside Inclosure then head NW and slightly downhill. Cross ford on Ditchend Brook. (If ford is too deep you can head N along bank here for the bridge you crossed near the beginning of the walk.) Take path heading NW to ridge in front of you. Cross another ford and climb valley side. (You can head to The Fighting Cocks PH at this stage!)

(7) *Turn right* at top of hill at Godshill cricket ground and head NE on level grass and gravel tracks, or along escarpment for 800 metres to return to car park.

Consulting the map - John Thackray

11

MOLLY & GEOFF'S WALK
2. BRAMBLE HILL AND BRAMSHAW

Walk Length and Time: 10 kms (6 miles) 3½ hours
Starting Point: Shepherds Gutter car park, Map Ref: SU261153
Take B3079 at Junction 1 M27 (signed Fordingbridge) through Brook to Stock's Cross then left, signposted Bramble Hill Hotel. Car park on left just after hotel entrance. If it is closed, use Bramshaw Wood CP, Map Ref: 258173.

Points of Special Interest
This walk is on the northern edge of the Forest and goes through "natural woodland" of oak, beech and holly, many of the trees dating from about 1700. Bramble Hill Lodge (now the hotel) was the Groom-keeper's lodge for the Northern Bailiwick of the Forest; the keeper was appointed by the Master Keeper - a highly placed personage such as the Marquis of Winchester or the Lord of Wardour Castle - to care for the "vert and venison" i.e. forest and deer. The building is now largely Victorian but inside can be seen remnants of medieval and Tudor features.
Bramshaw Wood provided timber for the building of Salisbury Cathedral and the parish is the only Forest parish in the diocese of Salisbury. A memorial in the church records the sad loss of seven young men of the parish, who were emigrating to a better life in America but perished on the Titanic.
The walk then traverses parts of Plaitford and Penn Common, an important area of bog and heathland given to the National Trust by the Eyre Family. Common rights are still practised as evidenced by the cattle, pigs and sheep turned out at various times of the year. The Warrens estate in Bramshaw was purchased by the Eyre family in 1798; from 1723 they had the right to print the Bible and Book of Common Prayer as the King's Printer. In 1812 George Eyre provided a school for the village. The Infant and Girls' School stood near the corner of Vice Lane and Stocks Lane, the Boys' department at the other end of the village near the church, but were amalgamated in 1900 when Mr George Briscoe Eyre built a new school. Stock's Cross was where the village stocks and gibbet stood - a very public place of punishment.

Walking Instructions
✳ From car park go back to the road and *turn right* to the driveway of Bramble Hill Hotel. (Some parts of the walk can be very muddy after wet weather.)
(1) *Turn left* and walk up drive to hotel. Just before it a footpath sign points *left*. Follow this gravel track past the stables and cottages to The Clock House. *Turn left* and go through a gate onto the open forest.

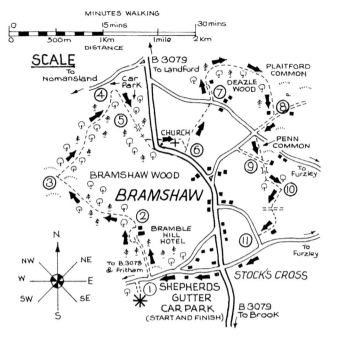

(2) At a bridleway/ footpath sign take the footpath (the bridleway tends to be muddier!). After 40 metres the path **bears left** in a westerly direction (DO NOT go straight ahead down the slope) going parallel with the bridleway. The path emerges on to a gravel track (linking with bridleway) which you follow in a generally westerly direction, ignoring any side paths, through a mixed deciduous woodland, coming out on the open heath after about 15 minutes (1 km) from the gate. The path is now a wide grassy track bearing right across the heath with heather on either side.

(3) The Nomansland road can be seen ahead, but well before you reach it turn right along the NW side of a shallow valley and head in a northerly direction. (Good views over the Test Valley in the distance.) Go through an old gravel pit and **keep bearing right** until you get into Bramshaw Wood. The well-worn path goes downhill through the woodland of mature oaks and beeches. Near the bottom of the hill the path goes **left then right** to cross a stream, which can be quite full in wet weather, and carry on down keeping an ancient forest bank on left. The path(s) now go up an incline to Bramshaw Wood car park (½ km - about 10 minutes). This is about one hour from the start of the walk without stops. (You can start the walk from here if Shepherd's Gutter CP is closed.)

(4) If you wish to visit the pub at Nomansland, 5mins away, turn left after car park. Otherwise, as Bramshaw Wood car park comes in sight, take the sharp **right fork** before the open green, and continue SE gently downhill through bracken and younger trees, to the bridge and carry on.

(5) Where the main track takes a turn to the left, **go straight ahead** on a path which is sometimes grassy, sometimes sandy. Go straight across the next track, following a somewhat eroded path but you soon see a footbridge in the valley below. Cross this and continue SE to reach a broad grassy path crossing in a glade. Turn left along this to Bramshaw-Landford road in about 150 metres. Cross onto gravel track (signed Vicarage Cottage only) and follow this, passing Vicarage Cottage, to a stile at the end of the now grassy path north of the church. Cross the stile and turn right. Then follow the hedge line up the slope, climb another stile into the cemetery and go along the path between the old cemetery wall and new hedge.

(6) Go over the stile into field and then sharp left and walk *diagonally NE* up the field (ignore path to left) to the stile at the far corner. The path now follows the hedge line and after climbing over 6 stiles you join a road where you turn left and almost immediately cross over into a "No Through Road".

(7) Go down the tarmac lane which becomes a gravelled forest track until you come out on the heathland of Plaitford Common. Bear *right* to skirt around the edge of Deazle Wood in an easterly direction, gradually turning SE and S.

(8) Cross 3 small footbridges before emerging on to a farm track past Paddock Cottage. Carry on along the lane until you reach a track, look back to see "The Hollies". Cut diagonally across Penn Common (NT), heading for the farm buildings at the SE corner. (A footbridge crosses the ditch about 20 metres in from the hedge line if needed in wet weather.) You will have taken about 2 hours to here.

(9) Leave Linhay Farm on your left and *turn left* at the fence corner. After 25 metres *go right* over stile into the woods and *fork left* at waymarked path to a footbridge and stile into a field. *Turn right* following the field edge for 400 metres.

(10) Before the field corner a footpath sign points *right* over a footbridge. Cross this, turn left, then skirt the field to a stile into the farm track. Go over the stile opposite and along a fenced path to the lane (Vice Lane).

(11) *Turn left* and then *right* at the tarmac road. Cross the B3079 on Stock's Common (NT) and walk straight ahead for 1 km (¾ mile) along the lane back to the car park (about 15 minutes).

Red Shoot wood - Robin Fletcher CA

14

ROY'S WALK
3. FRITHAM AND HIGH CORNER

Walk Length and Time: 13 kms (8 miles) 4¼ hours
Starting Point: Cadman's Pool Car Park, Map Ref: SU229123
From Ringwood turn left off A31 at Stoney Cross (signed Fritham) then left
(Linwood) at first junction. 1st car park on right.   From Lyndhurst take Emery
Down road at Swan Green. Turn left at pub (signed Bolderwood). On for 6 kms
(4 miles), under A31 then take first right. Car Park is on left. **Note: No right turn
off A31 at Stoney Cross.**

Points of Special Interest
This walk is largely across open areas of the Forest with fine views and is especially
attractive in the late summer when the heather is in bloom. Cadman's Pool (restored
in 2006) is one of only two ponds in the New Forest where fishing is allowed and is
on the edge of the old wartime airfield at Stoney Cross.   The walk passes through
Islands Thorns Inclosure which usually sees much commercial forestry activity. In
the autumn, it is quite common to see piles of wood stacked at the side of the track
for collection by those commoners who have the right to take fuelwood, known as
"Estovers". The walk then climbs up onto Hampton Ridge which is in the Ashley
Walk - a Walk being an old administrative area of the Forest. This area was also
used as an extensive bombing range during World War II and some signs are still
evident - a brick observation post, the only one still existing, and a mock up of
Submarine Pens (see Walk 1B) can be seen from the walk. The section of the walk
from the Submarine Pens to Hasley Inclosure and onto the High Corner Inn has
some particularly fine open views across Latchmore Bottom to Frogham, Hampton
Ridge and the hills of Wiltshire in the distance. The walk goes to the High Corner
Inn, situated in the heart of the Forest, for a well-earned rest and respite from the
elements in the winter. In keeping with most walks in the Forest, **some parts
can be very wet in the winter** and suitable footwear is advised, especially at the
beginning and end of the walk near Cadman's Pool.

Walking Instructions
✳ Pass through wooden barrier at the far W end of car park taking track which
bears slightly right. After l00 metres keep left in a westerly direction ignoring track
to right. Continue ahead gradually descending across a grassy area, which can be
wet at times, to the bottom and as far as the Inclosure fence. Turn right and follow
the path through the trees, with a ditch and fence soon appearing on the left, to the
corner of Holly Hatch Inclosure. *Turn left* and follow obvious path with fence on

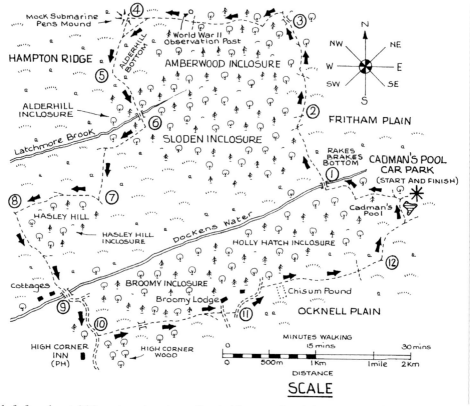

SCALE

left for about 200 metres to a long footbridge on the right over Dockens Water.

(1) *Turn right* to cross the bridge and follow the track which gradually climbs N of NW with open view on the right across Rakes Brakes Bottom towards Fritham Plain. At wooded area on the left keep straight ahead in the same direction with the open area of Fritham Plain on the right. The path levels out and soon meets a broad gravel track. Cross this and in 25 metres cross another gravel track.

(2) *Bear right* N to follow grassy path between the bracken with views to left towards Coopers Hill in the distance. At diagonal cross track in about 250 metres and *bear left* to descend gradually toward trees. Continue generally downhill through trees ignoring all cross tracks. On leaving the area of trees, with Islands Thorns Inclosure ahead, bear slightly *right* (ignore track bearing left towards gate posts and into Inclosure) to follow path across short open area to enter southern edge of Inclosure on a broad ride. Continue ahead to meet a gravel track. Keep straight ahead on this track to cross a footbridge.

(3) *Bear left* keeping on main track. (This is one of the places where fuelwood used to be stacked for collection. See page 15.) Follow the main track for about 750 metres gradually climbing and ignoring all tracks to the left into the Inclosure. Where

16

the track levels out continue ahead noting the remains of a brick observation post away on the right. Keep straight ahead W on the gravel track which crosses an open area with extensive views on both sides. At fork in about 400 metres take the *left* gravel track. Shortly after on the right is the mound of the Submarine Pens. (See Walk 1B)

(4)　　It is worth a short detour for the view and a break. (You have now completed about a third of the walk, or just over 4 kms (2½ miles), which will have taken about an hour plus stops). Shortly after passing (4) about 300 metres from the previous fork at diagonal cross tracks, *bear left* SW (the track on the right comes from the Submarine Pens and if you have visited them you may well be coming along it).

(5)　　After about 400 metres, where the track reaches end of ridge, take the left-hand narrow stony path steeply downhill, with fine views to the right, to go across Alderhill Bottom - wet at times - and pass through gate into Alderhill Inclosure. Follow the track straight ahead, ignoring all cross tracks. Just before joining a gravel track, look to the right for a seat erected in memory of the wildlife photographer Eric Ashby. After joining the gravel track, cross the bridge and go through the gate ahead to the grassy area between Alderhill Inclosure and Sloden Inclosure.

(6)　　*Turn right* SW and then after 500 metres, opposite corner of Alderhill Inclosure, cross a small stream and *turn left* to follow a path S gradually uphill across heathland towards Hasley Inclosure with good views to the right across Latchmore to Hampton Ridge, Frogham and the hills of Wiltshire.

(7)　　*Turn right* when reaching Hasley Inclosure onto a wide sandy track. Continue on this track with the edge of Inclosure on the left. On top of the ridge, where the main track bears right, *keep left* onto a path which generally runs S of W parallel to the northern edge of Inclosure with a fine view ahead, to reach the corner of the Inclosure after about 500 metres.

(8)　　*Turn left* to pass through a group of trees, keeping close to western edge of the Inclosure on the left, towards trees on a small ridge. Where the edge of the Inclosure turns left, keep straight ahead then immediately *bear slightly right* at eastern edge of the trees to join a sandy track. *Turn left* and follow track in a SE direction across valley bottom towards thatched white cottage ahead. Keep ahead across Woodford Bottom towards the fence of a small cottage to the left of the white cottage. Where a path joins from the right, *turn left* onto dirt path, passing the cottage on right.

(9)　　Cross the footbridge over Dockens Water to reach a track. *Turn left* onto this track which immediately bears right in a southerly direction for about 400 metres to reach the High Corner Inn. You have now completed about two-thirds of the walk, or about 9 kms (5½ miles).

(10)　　Retrace steps for 150 metres to open grassy area with a track on the left.

Turn right onto this grassy area to take a narrow path ahead through the trees. ***Bear slightly left,*** E, with the main wood on the right, across grass, then slightly right following a vague path (do not enter main wood). A grassy path gradually descends to cross a footbridge with Broomy Inclosure on the left. Go straight ahead and gradually uphill on grassy path keeping the Inclosure fence on the left. Where grassy path bears right at the top of the ridge, ignore it to keep ahead onto another grassy path towards telegraph poles at a gravel track leading into Broomy Lodge. Cross this and keep ahead, with a wooden fence on the left, to reach a second gravel track.

(11) ***Turn left*** onto this track gradually descending. Where it turns left to enter the Inclosure at a Forestry Commission sign for Holly Hatch Cottage Only, ***turn right*** past wooden barrier and Chisum Pound (this is one of the pounds used at the time of the annual drift or round-up of the Forest ponies) keeping the Inclosure fence on the left. The path then climbs to pass through a belt of trees and bears right away from fence. Keep on obvious path across open area of Ocknell Plain. After about 1 km from the pound, keep straight at cross tracks - path to left leads into the Inclosure - towards car park at Cadman's Pool.

(12) After about 400 metres, where the path divides, ***bear left*** onto narrow path through the heather towards old concrete strip. Just after reaching this, ***turn left*** to pass the pool on the right and return to car park.

DEREK AND MARIE'S WALK
4. BLASHFORD LAKES AND ROCKFORD COMMON

Walk Length and Time: 6½ kms (4 miles) 2½ hours
Starting Point: National Trust car park Rockford Common
near Moyles Court School Map Ref: SU164083. From Ringwood, go N
on A338. After 3 kms (2 miles) turn right signed Moyles Court.
First right, over bridge, then left and uphill to the car park on left.

Points of Special Interest
As in many parts of the New Forest, the RAF, USAF and other flying crews served
on wartime airfields in the area of this walk. A memorial to those based at the
nearest one, Ibsley Airfield, is situated in Ellingham Drove, not far from Moyles
Court School which boards many children whose parents are in the services.
Moyles Court was once the home of Alice Lisle, who was tried at the Bloody
Assizes and beheaded for harbouring some of Monmouth's rebels. There is a bust
of her in the Houses of Parliament, and the public house, which bears her name, is
seen in the early stages of the walk. It offers good food and pleasant views over one
of Blashford Lakes. Blashford Lakes are sites of former gravel extraction, which
is still going on locally. They are a major wildlife site which is heavily used by
internationally migrating birds, particularly in Spring and late Autumn.
Some of the cottages on this walk are quite charming, with pretty gardens, often
hidden in the most unexpected places. Their names also help to identify some often
obscure locations in this area of the forest.
Towards the end of the walk, as height is gained, there are pleasant views of Dorset
and Wiltshire to the west and north, including Cranborne Chase. A distant view of
Somerley, the Wyatt-designed home of the Earl and Countess of Normanton, can be
seen when returning to the car park. Both the house and gardens are occasionally
open to the public.

Walking Instructions
✳ Walk downhill from the car park along the verge in a westerly direction. (Moyles
Court School is ahead of you, across the stream.) ***Turn left*** before the stream along
the bank and cross the next road on your ***right.*** You are on the Avon Valley Path
(AVP).
(1)   Climb the metal stile on the ***left***, marked AVP. There are two wooden
footpath signs, take the one slightly to the ***left.*** Continue to the end of this path and
climb the stile near the Alice Lisle Public House. Keeping to the verge with the pub
on your ***right,*** continue over the cattle grid.

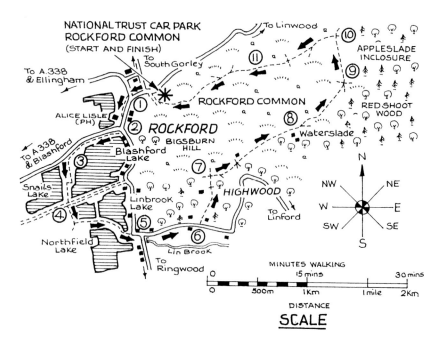

(2) Pass Ivy Lane on the right and in 25 metres *turn right* along a bridleway, just past a house. This path runs parallel to Ivy Lane and follows the edge of Blashford Lake, used by the Spinnaker Sailing Club.

(3) Continue to the Clubhouse and *turn left* at the footpath sign, through a gate. Keeping the lake on your left, proceed quite a long way to the kissing gate into a gravel road, Snails Lane.

(4) *Turn right* and in 50 metres *turn left,* still following the Avon Valley Path. Eventually *turn left* and follow the power lines. There is a small lake on the left and a winterbourne stream Lin Brook on the right.

(5) At the tarmac road *turn right.* In 30 metres *turn left* into a No Through Road signed for Highwood, keeping the stream on the right. Continue along this road, passing Heron Brook Bungalow, Oaks Farm, Linmore Cottage and Bracken Hill Cottage.

(6) *Turn left* up a track between two houses called Exley and Linbrook Thatch. This track is difficult to see as the footpath sign is hidden well round to the left. There is a beautiful new boardwalk (2010) over muddy stretches plus bridge. Continue along this and *bear left* at the first wooden five-barred gate. Continue uphill on the gravel track, leaving the house Tanglewood behind and go straight ahead at crossroads, due N.

(7) At next crossroads *turn right* around a bungalow called Foxglove Corner. Continue E down this track and go ahead past Lavender Farm and Yew Tree Cottage.

20

Keep ahead at next crossroads, leaving Mount Farm on your left. Pass Furzie Field on right and go uphill on earth track. Continue ahead NE. The path becomes indistinct through birch woodland here. Waterslade Farm is on the right. (However you cannot see a sign for the farm itself, although it is clearly marked on the map.)

(8) **Bear left** and continue to the gravel track and **turn left,** heading N.

(9) After 50 metres continue ahead to National Trust Land as the gravel track swings **left.**

A Helping Hand - Jim Hotchkiss

(10) At the top of the second small rise, **turn left** at path crossing. Head SW for about 1 km (½ mile) to reach a very extensive area of lower land (ancient gravel workings) and fork right around S.

(11) There is a view of Somerley House to the west. Leave the workings by a tarmac path going downhill to return to the National Trust Car Park.

A Rare Sight - Derek Higbee

ALAN & MARGARET'S WALK
5. ACRES DOWN AND HIGHLAND WATER INCLOSURE

Walk Length and Time: 8 kms (5 miles) 3 hours
Starting Point: Acres Down Car Park, Map Ref: SU267097
NW of Lyndhurst signposted to Emery Down off the A35 or 2 kms (1¼ miles) off the A31 from Cadnam. To reach Car Park go up lane opposite Newtown road and past tea rooms.

Points of Special Interest

This walk includes both the open heathland of the New Forest and enclosed woodlands. Near the start, walking on the sandy path, after passing Acres Down House, you will see on your left a tall stand of pines shading an old marl pit. Marl is a mixture of mud and lime, which was dug out of pits and spread on fields to counteract acid soils, both for arable and grass areas. The use of marl was an ancient and widespread practice, which retained an important role in improved farming through to the 19th century, when supplies of cheaply transportable lime became available. You will find these pits throughout the Forest where 'the right of marl' is still possessed by some Commoners.

Marling was a skilled craft with a host of technical terms, songs, customs and sayings attached to it. Two sayings were 'he that marls moss shall have no loss' and 'he that marls clays flings all away'. Gangs of marlers went from farm to farm, one of whom was chosen as 'Lord of the Soil'. Passers-by were asked for money and at the end of the week there was a celebration at the local inn. When a whole area was finished, everyone joined in - marlers, farmworkers, neighbours and tenants - there were drinks for all, songs, dancing and no doubt a good supper as well.

The seat before the trig point is a memorial with interesting inscriptions to the Burnett family and good advice, 'O sit still and look long and hold yourself quiet' (1). The inscription on the white stone at Murray's Passage (3) reads: - "This passage was made in memory of Thomas Murray who was killed hunting in the New Forest on 27 September 1901 on Backley Plain".

Keep a lookout for the many deer and numerous birds. Beware that under plans for the Forest, large swathes of conifers are being progressively felled to restore heathland and bogs over a twenty year period. Some gates and fences are also being removed. At the end of your walk you can always spoil yourself at "Annie's" with a cream tea (open from Good Friday until the end of September).

Walking Instructions

✳ Leaving Car Park **turn right** on gravel track to Acres Down House.
(1) **Turn left** passing the house and small bungalow on your right. Go N for 15mins to sandy path and gateway on your left. Go through gateway and onto cleared wood. Ignore path on left and **bear right** to T- junction. **Turn right** uphill passing

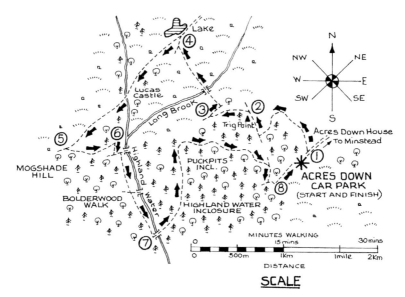

a seat on your right to open gateway and trig point on left.

(2) *Turn left* at the grassy cross paths and go in a NW direction. Walk along this path until you see the drift pens (temporary pony pens of logs) on the left.

(3) *Turn sharp right* on gravel track in NE direction. In 3 - 4 mins take the first left grass track down to Long Brook and Withybed Bottom (Murray's Passage), with good views of open forest and the A31 on the horizon. Go over footbridge and past inscribed stone. Continue uphill to T-junction and Model Yacht Lake (750 metres).

(4) *Turn left* in a SW direction and follow this path towards and to right of pine woods at Lucas Castle hill. Carry on downhill, over stream and then uphill passing gas line marker on the left by boggy stream. Mogshade Hill is in the distance.

(5) *Take first path left* near top of hill. Carry on downhill with trees and boundary on your right until you reach a small gate on your right. You are now about halfway round the walk and will probably have taken about 1½ hours, including short stops.

(6) Go through the gate into woodland on short path to junction, *turn left and immediately right.* Continue straight on in a SE direction on wide man-made grassy path, until a gravel path comes in on your right. Join the gravel track and proceed to the bridge over Highland Water (1 km).

(7) Go over bridge, *left* uphill NE on a grassy path and on gravel path to 5 path junction at the edge of Puckpits Inclosure. *Cross and turn right* on second path now heading alternately E and S. Carry on along the meandering, undulating path for 1½ kms to T-junction with cycle way marker.

(8) Turn left N through the gate and continue uphill to car park on your right.

23

REG & HILDA'S WALK

6. KNIGHTWOOD OAK AND HOLIDAYS HILL

Walk Length and Time: 8 kms (5 miles) 3 hours
Starting Point: Millyford Bridge Car Park, Map Ref: SU268078
Turn off A35 at Swan Green and take Emery Down road. Bear left at New Forest Inn (signed Bolderwood). Car Park is on right after 2 kms (1¼ miles).

Points of Special Interest
At the beginning of the walk there is a restored Portuguese Fireplace. It marks the area where there were huts for Portuguese soldiers who helped manage the Forest during the First World War. Camping is no longer allowed on Holidays Hill. Holidays Hill Inclosure has now been thrown open to Commoners' animals. It was one of the first to be made in the Forest in 1676, after a Royal Commission was appointed in 1670 to report on the state of the Forest, which had been neglected during the Civil War, and 300 acres were enclosed as a nursery for young oaks. One of the survivors from even before those days is now the most famous tree in the forest, the Knightwood Oak and it can still be seen near Point 2 on this walk. It has a girth of 7.5 metres (24 feet) and is probably 4-600 years old. It has a many-branched crown which indicates it has been pollarded or the main trunk of the tree was cut or broken off at a height of about 6m (20 feet) when the tree was young. After visiting the old oak tree, look nearby for one of the most fascinating sights in the forest. Two trees, an oak and a beech, have grown up fused together, known botanically as inosculation. This can happen with trees of the same species but is not usual with trees of a different species. Also in the same area there is an oak tree planted by Her Majesty the Queen in 1979 to mark the ninth centenary of the New Forest, and another planted by the Duke of Edinburgh in 1988. At the New Forest Reptile Centre, the Forestry Commission have a collection of breeding amphibians and reptiles native to the Forest. Frogs, lizards, slow worms and adders can be viewed safely, except in winter when most species hibernate.

Walking Instructions Note: Gates and fences are being removed and there has been much tree felling and clearance in some areas.
✴ From the car park walk back to the road and cross over, ***turn right*** and walk past the Portuguese Fireplace.
(1) Proceed to a gate on the left and a gravel track leading into Holidays Hill Inclosure. Go through the gate and keep to the right-hand track (ignoring the first fork). Follow it in a southerly direction for about 0.5 km (⅓ mile) until the track divides, and take the left-hand earthen track immediately ahead. Cross a pipe bridge over a stream, then follow the path uphill through a pine wood to a minor road

24

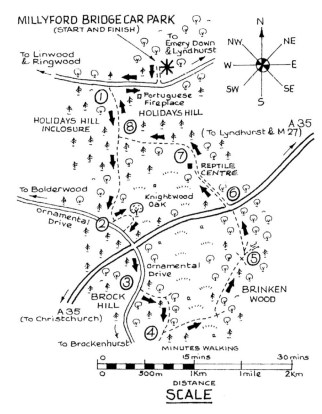

MILLYFORD BRIDGE CAR PARK
(START AND FINISH)
To Emery Down & Lyndhurst
To Linwood & Ringwood
Portuguese Fireplace
HOLIDAYS HILL
HOLIDAYS HILL INCLOSURE
(To Lyndhurst & M 27)
A 35
REPTILE CENTRE
To Bolderwood
Knightwood Oak
Ornamental Drive
Ornamental Drive
BROCK HILL
A 35 (To Christchurch)
To Brockenhurst
BRINKEN WOOD

N   NW   NE   W   E   SW   SE   S

MINUTES WALKING
15 mins   30 mins
500m   1Km   1mile   2Km
DISTANCE
SCALE

(Bolderwood Ornamental Drive). The Knightwood Oak Car Park is now opposite.

(2) Turn left and follow the signs to see this very old oak tree. Return to the road and *turn left* down the Ornamental Drive to the A35 (Lyndhurst to Christchurch) road. Cross this busy road and continue southerly along the Rhinefield Ornamental Drive and cross a bridge over a stream.

(3) After a short distance go through a gate on the left and follow the track which eventually bends round to the right. At the next cross tracks turn left and continue through a gate into Brinken Wood.

(4) After crossing a bridge over a stream, follow the main green ride which bears to the left through the birches. (Avoid the track straight ahead). It may be very wet in winter. Walk through the woods to a bridge over Highland Water without crossing it.

(5) *Turn left* to follow the stream in a northerly direction either on the bank or the path which runs parallel with it. Highland Water stream leads back to the A35. On reaching the road via the stream track, *bear left* for a short distance to a stile by a gate leading to the main road.

(6) Cross the road and walk through the entrance to the former Holidays Hill camp site. Follow the track to the Keeper's Cottage, and go through the gate beside the cattle grid and on to reach the Reptile Centre.

(7) After visiting, leave by the gravel track. After approximately 100 metres *turn left* on to a path. Follow this path through the woods to a gravel track. *Turn right* to follow the main track back to the gate at the start of the walk.

(8) *Turn right* at the road and walk past the Portuguese Fireplace back to the car park.

ANNE'S WALK
7A. LONGDOWN AND ASHURST WALK

Walk Length and Time: 8 kms (5 miles) 3 hours
Walks 7A and 7B start from the same point.
Starting Point: Deerleap Car Park, Map Ref: SU353094
Turn off A35 at Colbury down Deerleap Lane (1 km SW from A326 interchange). Car park is approximately 2 kms (1¼ miles) on right opposite New Forest Wildlife Park.

Points of Special Interest
This area of mixed woodland and open heath is seen to its best advantage in August when the heather and ling provides a purple carpet down to the Beaulieu River. If you approach the car park from the A35 you will pass Longdown Dairy Farm and the New Forest Wildlife Park, both of which are worthy of a visit.
As part of the long-term conservation plan for the New Forest, many areas of the Forest are having conifers removed, so heathland and valley mires/bogs can be restored. Longdown Inclosure has now been 'thrown open', all fencing and gates have been removed so commoners' animals and deer can now roam freely. The name Deerleap is said to commemorate an amazing death leap of more than 18 yards by a stag which had been shot. Two posts once marked the spot.

Walking Instructions
✳ From the car park head S along the ridge for 500 metres keeping Longdown on your left.
(1) Take the first *left hand*, easterly track. Follow this track for 625 metres to the third track on the right.
(2) *Turn right* and continue S for 600 metres to a T-junction.
(3) *Bear left* and S passing a gravel track coming in from the left.
(4) From here your path *bears right* and in a generally southerly direction for approximately 750 metres to a cross track.
(5) *Turn right,* SW, across the wooden bridge. Within 10 metres the path veers *right* and W and you should follow it for 500 metres to a cross track where you *turn left.*
(6) Continue S downhill towards the distant trees hiding the railway line. On your left you can see the chimneys of Fawley refinery. Follow the path downhill over the heath, a distance of some 650 metres, until you reach a cross track at the edge of the trees near Fulliford Passage. The walk continues along the right-hand path but, as you are about half way round, you may like to take a break in the shade by the river, in which case follow the track into the trees for a few metres.

26

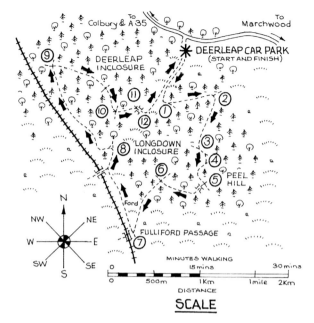

SCALE

(7) Returning to the path and keeping the railway line to your *left,* pick up the north-westerly track for the next 750 metres via a ford by a hedge. N.B. This ford is sometimes impassable in winter. In summer the area abounds in bog myrtle. Crush some leaves between your fingers and enjoy the aroma. Having crossed the ford, follow the path uphill towards Deerleap Inclosure. As you near Deerleap you will notice a railway bridge to your left. *Bear right* here, walk N for 100 metres and enter the Inclosure gate.

(8) Take the *left-hand* gravel track and head NW for about 1½ kms until you reach the second cross track by a cycle waymark.

(9) Ignoring the gravel track to your left, take the grassy ride to the *right.* This lush, often muddy, way is rich in tall grasses and wild flowers. Continue E for about 750 metres, over a cross track, to a conjunction of five paths.

(10) Cross the gravel track to the narrow, easterly path opposite.

(11) *Turn right* at the end of this track over a wooden bridge to the Inclosure gate, which is only about 400 metres (5 minutes).

(12) After leaving the Inclosure, *turn left* and follow the ridge NE for 750 metres to the car park.

Reflection - Vic Ruston

27

DOREEN AND TONY'S WALK
7B DECOY POND

Walk Length and Time: 7 kms (4½ miles) 3 hours
Walks 7A and 7B start from the same point.
Starting point: Deerleap Car Park, Map Ref: SU353094
For directions see previous walk.

Points of Special Interest
This is a good walk for summer, preferably in dry conditions when the Beaulieu River is fordable and the heather is out. An alternative route is given in case the river is too deep to ford, but even so boots are recommended as there are some muddy ponds. *Tony's Tip* – Plastic shopping bags without holes make excellent overboots to get you through the ford if the water is above boot height. Wellington boots are recommended in wet conditions.

This mainly heathland walk passes between and around two Verderers' Inclosures that were first planted in the 1960s with Scots pine. Much of the soil is too poor to sustain oak and the pine is now being progressively removed to restore heath and bogs. See Walk 7A.

The route passes Providence Wesleyan Methodist Chapel which served the hamlet of Longdown. There was also a school shown on the 1869 OS, map but now even the chapel is a private residence. Yew Tree Heath, after Pottern Ford on the Beaulieu River, is so called due to a large yew tree in existence when the Driver's first edition map of the New Forest was published in 1789.

Decoy Pond was created by Oliver Cromwell circa 1659 for duck hunting. The old London and SouthWestern Railway was built in 1846/47 and the New Forest section was the last to be built due to problems with wayleaves. The route crosses some typical New Forest lawns at Matley Holms before re-crossing the river – this time by a bridge. During the First World War an artillery range was created from Matley to Decoy Pond (1917), but this was changed to a War Dog Training School in 1918. It was soon closed following strong protests by the Verderers after local livestock was worried by the dogs when released to run messages back to Matley.

Walking Instructions
✳ Proceed from the lower car park in a SE direction for 400 metres following the path that runs parallel to the transmission lines on your right to a wooden bridge.
(1)   Continue over the bridge for 100m, then fork right and carry on for about 50 metres. (Longdown is no longer inclosed.)
(2)   *Turn left*, proceeding SE up a wide grassy ride which eventually leads to a

28

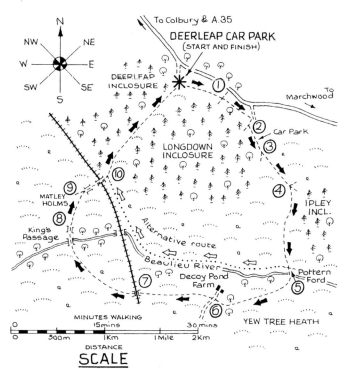

sandy/gravel path. The transmission lines should now be on the left. Pass through a stand of trees, and at the point where the sandy path bears left, continue straight ahead over grass to the top of the rise. *Cross* a gravel track and immediately *bear* SE through the trees to cross another car park (Longdown).

(3) To your left you may glimpse the old Wesleyan chapel through the trees. Head for the single bar gate and pick up the gravel track which runs by some gorse bushes in a southerly direction. After 150 metres the gravel track splits into two lesser tracks. Take the left-hand one that bears south of SE, passing through small hillocks and heading towards Ipley Inclosure in the distance. As you cross this open heathland, you can see Decoy Pond Farm through the distant trees on your right-hand side.

(4)   As you approach Ipley Inclosure the path forks – take the right-hand one, with a gorse bush on the right and skirting three pine trees on the left. This track peters out and you must now walk through a stand of trees with the main Inclosure fence on your left. From the centre of this stand of trees, turn S. When you reach the edge you will see a downhill path running across the heath. Follow the path towards the distant trees which border the Beaulieu River (Pottern Ford).

(5)   (*Start of alternative route) Cross the river and walk forward through the green ride until you reach open heathland (Yew Tree Heath). Turn right and proceed in a SW direction, angling away from the river and generally heading for the southern end of a copse directly in front of you. Gradually swing W (no clear tracks). (Ignore the path that you can see on the hill - left). Shortly, you will pick up a defined path leading towards the copse. Follow this path and enter the wood with a large oak tree to your right. The path bears right and you will now see the buildings

29

on your right through the trees.

(6) A large fallen tree provides a good sitting place to have your halfway rest. Continue past the farm buildings in a westerly direction following the path, which joins a metalled road by a bungalow for approximately 50 metres. The metalled road bears left by Decoy Pond farmhouse. Continue straight ahead into the trees - take either of the two footpaths, which rejoin further ahead. On emerging from the trees you see high ground to the left (Black Down), open heath in front and trees away to the right (Withycombe Shade). Follow the path directly across the heathland – heading for the railway bridge.

(7) Pass under the bridge and follow a path in a NW direction heading for one of the forest lawns. After 100 metres, the gorse and heathland run out and you are on the edge of the lawn. Keeping in the same NW direction, cross the lawn leaving a hedgerow and fern to your right. There is no distinct path so aim to bisect the further edge of the lawn in the middle, where you will find a wide, distinct footpath leading to a clearly visible footbridge (King's Passage).

(8) After crossing a second footbridge, go straight on, uphill, for a few metres to another lawn (Matley Holms). Follow the footpath across the lawn in a northerly direction. You now have the railway over to your right.

(9) As you approach the river the path bears right to bridge the river and continues up to bridge the railway.

(10) Cross the railway bridge and proceed straight ahead through a stand of trees with Deerleap Inclosure to your left. The wide gravel path runs parallel to the Inclosure fence and eventually splits into two paths. Follow the left-hand one which leads directly back to the higher car park.

(*)Alternative route

Fly Agaric - Vic Ruston

Confirm depth of water and if too deep backtrack approximately 50 metres to find a small footpath, which runs in a W direction parallel to the river and outside of the trees. This path meanders along following the course of the river but it stays outside the trees. There are some muddy patches, but normal walking boots will get you through. The path eventually begins to swing in a NW direction and you will see a bridge (Fulliford Passage) under the railway to your left. Continue on the footpath which begins to swing N until it joins the original route by the railway bridge **(10)**. Follow the main route description back to the car park.

ANNE AND TREVOR'S WALK
8 PIG BUSH - YEW TREE HEATH AND KING'S HAT

Walk Length and Time: 9 kms (5½ miles) 3¼ hours.
Starting Point: Take train to Beaulieu Road Station and walk, or drive to Pig Bush Car Park at Map Ref: SU362051on B3056 Beaulieu to Lyndhurst road.

Points of Special Interest
This walk is in the collecting area for the middle section of the Beaulieu River, so in parts it can be wet underfoot.
In contrast, it crosses a much drier area on one of the Forest lawns at Gurnetfields Furzebrake, and alongside a second dry area by Aldermoor Lodge. These areas (lawns) provide higher quality grazing for ponies and deer. We also skirt round Ferny Crofts, now an activity centre owned by Hampshire Scouts. Previously it was cottage dwellings, but in medieval times it was owned by Beaulieu Abbey and frequented by the monks. On its western perimeter we pass a rather eerie pond in the trees, (see picture p 27). Apparently it was formed relatively recently by small scale gravel extraction, possibly used in the concrete for the anti-aircraft gun position at what is now Yew Tree Heath car park.

Walking Instructions: ✳Start from Pig Bush Car Park, about 20 mins walk SE from Beaulieu Road Station along B3056.
(1) *Cross* the road (B3056) out of car park and head for clump of trees on your *right*. Pick up the path running NE skirting the left hand side of some trees and bushes. This path curves round to the right and runs E about 10-20 metres away from a fence on your right. This is the perimeter fence of Culverley Farm. About 500 metres from the road, look out next for a path going off to your left.
(2) Turn *left* (N) on to this good gravel path through some boggy terrain. It crosses a small wooden bridge, then climbs up onto open heathland, coming to woodland on your right. In the sparse trees the pond is now rather overgrown, but have a look. Return onto the path and continue to follow it N and then E around the pond and boundary until reaching the gravel access road to Ferny Crofts, and then turn *left* following the road away from the house.
(3) On reaching a tarmac road, *cross over* and follow the concrete road N to Yew Tree Heath car park. At the end of the concrete and at the Forestry Commission post, turn *right* from the car park across the open heath heading towards power lines in the far distance.
(4) After 500 metres turn *right* on reaching a crossing path running W-E. Fawley Refinery chimneys are now ahead of you on the skyline. This sandy path running east takes you to the perimeter trees around Aldermoor Lodge lawn. Follow along

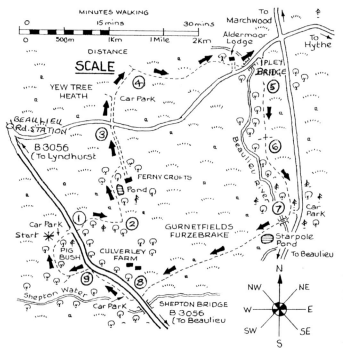

this line of trees and you will come to the road. Join the road, turning **left,** and follow along the roadside for a very short distance crossing the bridge over the Beaulieu River. Pass Ipley Manor gateway on the left. Shortly after, cross the road and turn *right* onto the heath at the end of the dragon's teeth. (There used to be a car park here.)

(5) Head south across the heath keeping close to the trees on your right. In about 200 metres you need to cross a small stream, which is normally no problem in boots, and continue heading S. About 300 metres from the stream the path divides into two, and the one you want goes off to the *left* heading SE away from the trees and onto the open heath.

(6) After about 200 metres a path crosses over E-W. Keep on the existing path, now heading S, and in about 300 metres cross a narrow but deeper stream. By moving up or down stream about 10-20 metres, you can find some tussocks to use as stepping stones. Continue just east of S for 400 metres heading for King's Hat car park. **There is no defined path for much of section 7-8.**

(7) Turn *right* and follow the gravel path SW through trees down to the wooden footbridge spanning the Beaulieu River. After a pause at this atmospheric spot, cross the bridge, climb the bank and you are once again on open heath. Proceed straight ahead SW up the slightly inclined ground for about 300 metres until reaching a level grassy area, often with forest animals grazing. This is Gurnetfields Furzebrake. Cross this grassy lawn SW, aiming between trees on the left and right horizons, to an area of gorse and bracken, in the centre of which you should discern a grassy path going SW. Follow this, still going in the same direction, for about 500 metres until reaching a gravel road going SW. Turn *left* here onto the gravel road, which in about 200 metres brings you to a tarmac road, the B3056 Beaulieu-Lyndhurst road at Shepton Bridge.

32

(8)   Cross the B3056, leaving Shepton Water on your left, and turn *right* (NW) and follow the uphill gravel track into Culverley car park. The B3056 road is about 50 metres away on the right, and for the next 300 metres your track runs parallel to it.

(9)   You then arrive at a dip, alongside the road, and at this point turn *left* onto a path going W away from the road. This path curves around the outside of Pig Bush Wood. **(Ignore the very well defined path going off to the left SW about 200 metres from the road.)** Having followed this path round Pig Bush wood for about 500 metres, turn *right* into any suitably clear part of the wood. Finally, climb upwards for about 200 metres to reach Pig Bush car park alongside the B3056.

VIC AND ROSE'S WALK
9. BURBUSH AND DUR HILL

Walk Length and Time: 6½ kms (4 miles) 2½ hours
(Excluding optional extra of 0.8km (½ mile) to look at Thorney Hill Church)
Starting Point: Burbush Hill car park, Map Ref: SU202018
Turn off A31 at Picket Post to Burley. In the village turn right to follow Bransgore Road (south). Car park is on left about 1.5 kms (1 mile) from village centre. Or N from Bransgore, Car Park is on right just after disused railway track.

Points of Special Interest
The car park, and start of the walk is at the side of the former railway line known as Castleman's Corkscrew because of the devious route it had to follow. The line opened in June 1847 and was closed in the mid 1960s "Beeching Axe". The first part of the walk follows the former railway line for a short distance. The walk is mainly on well-defined tracks and covers a range of habitats: wide open areas, sheltered sections and a little woodland, plus some fine views towards the Avon Valley - a walk that anyone interested in natural history should enjoy. The route passes close to Bagnum Bog and most of the Forest bog plants can be found in the vicinity. A good variety of butterflies and many birds live in the sheltered stretches. Whitten Pond is a favourite spot for many of the forest animals and at certain times large numbers of Canada geese can be seen paddling around. The outfall from the pond finds its way to the Avon Water and out to the sea at Keyhaven.
Thorney Hill Church was built about 1908 by the Manners family. It has had its share of misfortune. Almost screened from view by Scots pine surrounding it, the gales of 1990 brought most of them down and local people took on the task of clearing up the mess. Now replanted with ornamental trees and shrubs. The lead was stolen from the roof and during repairs the roof caught fire, but was saved by the quick action of the local Fire Brigade. Note the cherubs on the front and back of the church, reputed to be a likeness to a member of the Manners family.
The Fortune Riding Centre is a residential centre for disabled people.

Walking Instructions
✳ From the car park entrance, cross the Burley/Bransgore road and head broadly W following the wide track almost opposite with the old railway line hidden in the trees on your left. The route wanders away from the railway to skirt small ponds that are sometimes dry in the summer. Up a small rise in the track and ahead is the hill named Brown Loaf. The path swings first right then left around the base of the hill and into the trees to a bridge over the old railway.

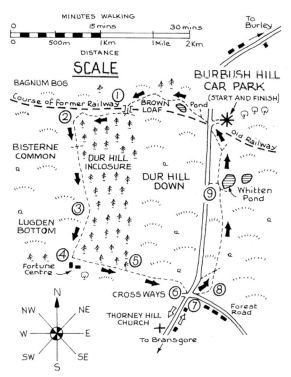

(1) This is about 1 km from the start of the walk. Cross the bridge and pass the holding pen on the right, used by the Commoners during the pony drifts. *Turn right* (W) and take the path through the trees (NOT the path through the old gateposts). The railway should now be on your right and the track is again a wide sandy one. It slopes gradually down until just before meeting the Forest boundary fence.

(2) This is approximately 400 metres from the bridge. The area on the other side of the fence is Bisterne Common, a very marshy area, while on the right beyond the line of the old railway is Bagnum Bog. Leaving the old railway behind us, the route *turns left* (S) over a series of small hillocks. We now have the Forest boundary fence on the right. The pines at Dur Hill are being cleared to recreate more heathland and this will be completed by 2020, but the boundary banks will remain. This is one of the so-called Verderers' Inclosures planted during the 1960s. Ignore any of the tracks going off to the right and left. The southern end of Dur Hill Inclosure has been felled.

(3) One km from where the route turned S, it swings right SW and goes uphill, still along the boundary of the Crown Lands.

(4) 400 metres after the bend and near the top of the rise the route *turns left* (SE) still following the boundary fence. On the right is a private area with riding stables (Fortune Riding Centre), etc. This is a nice spot for a break if required and about halfway round the walk. Continue with the fence close on the right.

(5) 600 metres from the turn, the Inclosure is left behind. We now have good views across the Forest to the Burley area. Our route goes straight ahead on a well-defined track, keeping the boundary fence on the right. This path dodges between the gorse and other bushes but keep within sight of the fence. We are heading towards the Bransgore/Burley road and approximately 100 metres from the road the path divides.

(6) Take the path to the right, which brings you to Crossways at Thorney Hill.

At this point the walk to see Thorney Hill Church is the optional extra (see 'Points of special interest'). It is 400 metres down the Bransgore road on the right. The Bransgore road is signposted. Return to Crossways.

(7) Cross the road to the nameplate, Forest Road. Behind this and just to the right is an open stretch of grassland. Go straight down the centre of this for only 60 metres.

Forest Resident - Vic Ruston

(8) *Turn left* onto an even wider area of grassland and again go down the centre. Direction is just to the E of N. In 85 metres you reach a large patch of gravel, and *turning left* around the gorse bushes should bring the gravel path going N into view. Looking ahead down the hill, Whitten Pond should be in sight and that is where you are heading. The Bransgore/Burley road is approximately 200 metres on the left and the path runs almost parallel to this.

(9) *Keep to the left* (W) side of the large pond and on the far side a sandy track heads towards the old railway. Where this track divides *go left* to the bridge over the old railway. Cross the bridge to the car park.

After prolonged wet weather keep closer to the road to avoid wet and mud near ponds.

Bogs have beauty - Archie Miles CA

36

DAVID AND BERNICE'S WALK
10. WOOTTON BRIDGE AND AVON WATER

Walk Length and Time: 8 kms (5 miles) 3 hours
Starting Point: Wootton Bridge car park, Map Ref: SZ251997
Turn off A35 at Holmsley (signed Brockenhurst). After 2 kms (1¼ miles) turn right. Car park is on right in about 200 metres.

Points of Special Interest
This interesting walk takes you through a less frequented part in the south-west of the Forest. It is reasonably dry in summer but the section from the start along Avon Water can be wet in winter.
First it follows the course of the Avon Water nearly as far as the A35 at Holmsley. It's a short detour to Holmsley Tea Rooms in the original Station on the old railway from Brockenhurst to Ringwood. The route then goes into Brownhill Inclosure which is now 'thrown open' with all gates and fences removed and a mixture of beech, oak, yew, holly and thorn. Skirting Little Wootton Inclosure, the south side of which is a strange wetland area, the route continues through the gravel roads of Wootton, a mixture of houses, paddocks and farms, and then enters Wootton Coppice Inclosure and returns to the car park at Wootton Bridge.

Walking Instructions
✻ Leave the car park and cross the road bridge to the far side of Avon Water. *Turn right* and follow a path close to the river bank. There are several small streams/ditches to cross and parts of the route may be muddy in wet weather especially in winter. Continue for approximately 1.5 kms (1 mile) until you see a tunnel on your right under the road. (*See footnote if wet underfoot.*)
(1) Ignore this and keep to the open ground between the river and the fenced Inclosure, then *bear left* to the fenced corner. If you wish to visit the Holmsley Tea Rooms you should head N to the corner of the open area, cross a bridge over the river, go to the right and then under the A35.
(2) To continue the walk without diversion, at the fence corner *turn left,* cross the ditch and enter the Inclosure through the gate on your left. Proceed uphill along the earth and grass ride. Bear *right* at the gravel track. In 50 metres bear *right* onto grassy path. In 300 metres *turn right* onto another gravel track, then almost immediately *left* and then *right* also on gravel tracks. ** See footnote.* Continue straight on through gate for about 1 km (½ mile), ignore track on the left and bear right at junction, then through car park to the road (B3058).
(3) Cross the road and go SW along the path outside Little Wootton Inclosure for ½ km (¼ mile) and on reaching gate posts on left go through.

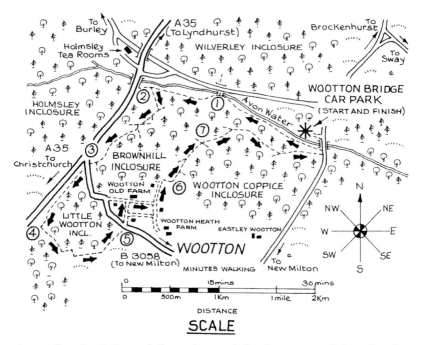

SCALE

Turn immediately right to follow the earth bank on your right. Continue until you reach a wide earth track near the corner of the Inclosure.

(4)	**Turn left** and keep alongside earthbank (to left of fallen trees). Where it becomes indistinct, **bear right** onto the open heath, and head for two blue signs. Take the path left and on reaching a gravel track **bear left** across the heath to the road at the corner of the Inclosure.

(5)	Cross it and go down Wootton Farm Road. At T-junction (Wootton Old Farm) **turn right.** At the next T-junction **turn left.** At the end of the gravel road cross ditch on to wide track and **turn right.**

(6)	Almost immediately go through gate on **left** into Wootton Coppice Inclosure and walk straight on. Ignore first path on right and join gravel track bearing **right.**

(7)	When you meet the gravel track at cycle marker 21 continue ahead down the path opposite with stream on your left. On joining the next gravel track, **bear right** and follow the main track keeping **left** at next junction. Go through the gate and **turn left** to Wootton Bridge car park.

Footnote. Conservation work has made the first part of this walk difficult for the less able. As an alternative beginning, you can go out onto the road. Turn right over bridge and right again to enter woods on gravel track, which goes right through for about 1½km (1 mile), ignoring all side paths, to * in section **(2)** of Walking Instructions.

AUDREY'S WALK
11. BROCKENHURST AND QUEEN BOWER

Walk Length and Time: 9 kms (5½ miles)   3¼ hours
Starting Point: Tilery Road (Balmer Lawn) car park, Map Ref: SU307034.
On N side of B3055, 500m E of A337, NE of Brockenhurst.

Points of Special Interest
This is an attractive and varied walk. The first part, along the upper reaches of the Lymington River, may be a little muddy after rain, but the rest is either on good paths or firm grass. The fields visible on the right during the first part of the walk belong to New Park, so designated by Charles II to distinguish it from the old Park around Lyndhurst. New Park was the King's favourite hunting lodge and he created the field system in 1670 as a Royal Deer Park. After Bolderford Bridge **(1)** the path goes through beautiful Queen Bower wood, a favourite place of Queen Eleanor, wife of Edward I, who lived at Lyndhurst in 1280 while her husband was off fighting the Welsh. Near the bridge, the Highland Water, Blackwater and Ober Water all combine to become the Lymington River. Halfway between points **(1)** and **(2)**, by a small bridge, there is a wooden seat (something quite rare in the Forest) which used to bear a plaque quoting lines from a poem by Robert Burns, in memory of another lady who loved this spot "till all the seas gang dry". When you reach point **(2)**, before turning left on to the gravel track, look across ahead and to the right to Queen's Meadow, a wide open space where you may well see some deer. Poundhill Inclosure was one of the last haunts of the red squirrel in the Forest. After passing point **(6)**, when walking across the wide expanse of Black Knowl heath, note the wavy character of the grassland, due to the land having been ploughed up during wartime for agriculture. Butts Lawn, just before point **(7)**, so named after the archery targets in the days when every man had to practise the use of the longbow.

Walking Instructions
✳From car park head W to A337, passing Balmer Lawn Hotel on your left. Cross A337 at entrance to Hollands Wood campsite and go through a gate or over stile. Follow path NW through woods bearing left at fork in 100m, keeping river on your left (although you may lose sight of it from time to time). Go over a small stream (no bridge) and carry on over a possibly muddy area. After going over a flat bridge and over another stream, fields will appear on your right. Keep by fence as this stretch can be muddy and uneven. After about half a kilometre, you will come to Bolderford Bridge on your left.

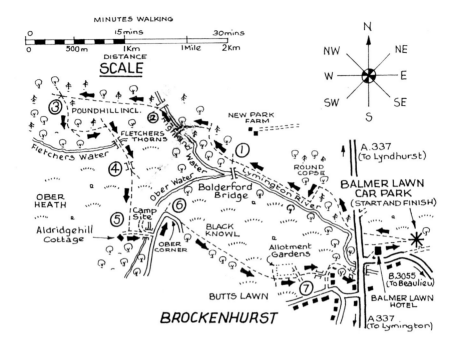

(1) *Do not cross the bridge, turn right and immediately left* on a narrow path, marked by a "No Cycling" sign. Keep the fence and ditch to your right and in about a kilometre you will come to a wooden seat and "Conservation Area" sign on left by a bridge. Cross this bridge and continue through beautiful woodlands with the river now on your right, for about half a kilometre, until you come to another small bridge at a T-junction.

(2) *Turn left* here and take the wide gravel path to a gate into Poundhill Inclosure. After going about a kilometre on this path, ignoring two cross paths, you will come to a junction of five paths. This will have taken you about 1 hour plus stops. You are about halfway round the walk.

(3) Take the first (sharp) *left-hand* track and after about half a kilometre leave the main track where it curves right and take a grassy path half-left to a gate, leading to open heath. Go straight on about 100 metres to another gate-sized gap in a fence and then on towards Fletchers Thorns. Turn right when you get to the hedge and you will see a river and bridge ahead (GR 498044).

(4) Cross the bridge and go straight on through a shrubby area on to the heath, and you will see a footbridge ahead. After crossing this footbridge, take the half-right grassy path towards a white house, Aldridgehill Cottage, a bit more than a kilometre away.

(5) Just before reaching the cottage, *turn left* onto the campsite road and keep

40

straight on *turning right* across the river bridge at the site entrance. *Turn left* on to the road or walk through the woods on the left of the road, until you come to a sign "Ober Corner".

(6) Leave the road here, head SE and walk along the line of the trees, keeping them 100/150m on your right, on a sometimes indistinct grassy path (Black Knowl). After about a kilometre, you will come to a raised gravel path roughly at right angles to the one you are on. *Turn right* E on this path and go up a slight rise, and you will see some allotments over to the left. Go along S side of the allotments' fence to its end, (Butts Lawn). Continue E along faint wide and grass track for about ½km and you will then see a steep gravelly track leading to a small river.

(7) Cross the footbridge and *turn immediately left* towards a row of cottages. Turn past the last on the left, leave the road and follow a narrow path E through woods, keeping the little river on your left. When very near the road, you will cross a small plank bridge. Then *turn right,* go through a kissing gate and up some steps on to the A337. *Turn left*, cross this road and the next (B3055) to pass in front of the Balmer Lawn Hotel, then *turn half - right* back to the car park.

DAVE AND GILL'S WALK
12. SETLEY POND AND ROYDEN WOODS

Walk Length and Time: 6½ kms (4 miles) 2½ hours
Starting Point: Setley Pond car park, Map Ref: SZ302992
From A337 3 kms (2 miles) S of Brockenhurst and 300 metres N of The Hobler, take Burley road. Car park is on the left.

Points of Special Interest
When you leave the car park, the heathland which you cross used to be a bog, hence moor. When you go down Church Lane, on the right-hand side you will see what is left of the Morant Racing Gallops. On the left-hand side is Tile Barn H.C.C. Outdoor Centre. St. Nicholas' Church, which is mentioned in The Domesday Book is worth a diversion. The churchyard has many First World War graves, including an Indian's headstone. A famous New Forest snake catcher, Brusher Mills (1838-1905), is also buried here. In his lifetime he is said to have caught between 30,000 and 35,000 snakes. He either sold his catch alive or rendered it down to fat selling the skeletons as ornaments. He claimed that one of his ointments made from adder fat would cure everything from black eyes to rheumatic joints and sore feet.
Royden Woods Nature Reserve contains a wonderful patchwork of habitats which supports wildlife typical of the New Forest without the pressures of grazing. It was gifted freehold to the Hampshire Wildlife Trust by Peter Barker Mill in 1978 and has been privately owned since the time of the Domesday Book.
Where you walk back along the gravel track towards the A337 road, there used to be a lot of Army huts. It was a very good place to hide the troops for the invasion of France.
When you get back on the Setley Plain, cast your mind back to World War II, as where you are walking was a German Prisoner of War camp.

Walking Instructions
✳ Leave the car park in a NW direction along a well-defined track to the road. Cross the road to the Forestry barrier and carry on NW towards the trees in the distance.
(1)   When you can see the roof of a house in the dip ahead, *bear right* on the track going NE, keeping right of the trees along the edge of a wood. *Turn left* and then down into a depression and onto the road. On reaching the road, cross straight over and *turn right* into Tilebarn Lane. Go over the cattle grid and walk along to the main A337 road. Cross straight over and walk up Church Lane, passing the HCC Outdoor Centre Tilebarn Camp, until you reach a bridleway on your right-hand side. (If you wish to visit St. Nicholas' Church carry on down the lane for about 200 metres.)

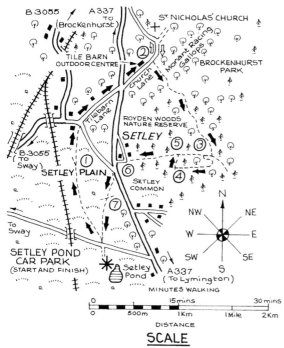

(2)   Follow the bridleway into Royden Nature Reserve and go through a gate. After about 1km go through another gate and carry on to a T-junction with a gravel track. *Turn right* at the bridleway sign onto the path for 30 metres to a kissing gate on your left. Go through the gate, *bearing left,* and follow the path on round.

(3)   Watch for a white topped marker post on the left and follow marked path to a 2nd marker post. *Turn left* down the path, going over a small plank footbridge. The path goes through the wood along an old forest Inclosure bank. Walk up a slight incline with telegraph poles on your left and fir trees to the right, over a second plank bridge and on up to a white post.

(4)   *Turn right* onto track through the pine wood and follow this round for about 300 metres to a kissing gate.

(5)   *Turn left* onto the gravel track and walk on to the main A337 road.

(6)   Cross over to the cattle grid and take the path on the left, ignoring paths on your right, to the open plain.

(7)   Head SW to a lone pine tree, to the left of which is a path heading S. Sway Tower can be seen in the distance. Follow the track back to the car park.

Testing the water - Jim Hotchkiss

43

GLYNIS AND FRANK'S WALK
13. LEPE AND INCHMERY

Walk Length and Time: 9 kms (5½ miles) 3¼ hours
Starting Point: Pull in on E side of Lepe Road, just S of Whitefield
Farm Business Units, Map Ref: SU449005. Take A326 S past Fawley Refinery and
then fork right towards Blackfield and Lepe. Car park is on right after nearly 4 kms
(2 ½ miles). The start of the walk can also be reached by Bluestar Bus. This walk
also incorporates part of the Hampshire County Council's "Lepe Loop".

Points of Special Interest
This area of the New Forest has many connections with the Second World War.
Lepe House, which was once a smuggler's inn, was part of HMS Mastoden, the main
part of which was at Exbury House. It was used by Special Operations Executive
(SOE) for training agents. A jetty and hard were built on the beach in front of Lepe
House for the supply of fuel and water to landing craft from tanks in the garden of
Lepe House. The remains of the hard can still be seen at low tide. Inchmery House
was requisitioned early in the war, and was used as a commando training school
for Polish and French troops. Further information can be found in the book "The
Beaulieu River Goes to War 1939 - 45" by Cyril Cunningham.
This walk takes you through very varied scenery - farmland, woodland and along
the foreshore of the Solent, with views of Gull Island Bird Sanctuary and the Isle of
Wight. Through the farmland, as well as crops, you are likely to see horses, cattle
and pigs. Where a number of the stiles are at the edges of fields not containing
animals, you may find that you can go round them rather than having to climb over
them. Parts of the walk can be muddy if the weather has been wet. Also part of
the foreshore section can be very difficult and slippery at high tide. An alternative
route is given to avoid this section if necessary.

Walking Instructions
✳ The walk starts just past Whitefield Farm Business Units on the Lepe Road.
Head along Lepe Road on the right-hand side of the road towards Lepe for 750
metres passing Darkwater House on your right.
(1)   *Turn right* along bridleway heading W. After 600 metres the bridleway
diverts to the right, but continue straight on along a footpath for 15 metres which
then turns left.
(2)   After 100 metres *turn left* along footpath crossing a small bridge heading
S. Continue up a hill for 150 metres to edge of field. Continue across next field
heading S. Go round a stile (with yellow marker) and continue across field

44

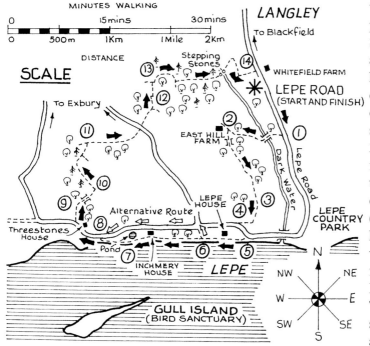

towards electricity pole still heading S. Then continue across the field heading SE to corner of wood on left. Continue straight on for 300 metres across field heading SSE towards middle electricity pole. **(3)** Go through kissing gate. You will now get your first view of the Isle of Wight and The Solent. Bear slightly *right* and after 150 metres go through gateway. Go over small concrete bridge and through gate. The footpath now bears round to the right, heading W.

(4) Go through kissing gate to road. *Turn left* and continue along road heading S for 150 metres. (Go left here for Lepe Country Park.)

(5) At seafront *turn right* down to shoreline footpath. Before going down to the shoreline you will see a Millenium Beacon to your right. You will now see Lepe House on your right. Continue along shoreline footpath heading W with views of the Isle of Wight to your left.

(6) After 400 metres an alternative footpath goes right. You may need to return to this footpath if a high tide makes the shoreline route too difficult (see later). Continue along shoreline for 600 metres. Inchmery House is now on your right.

(7) The next section can be difficult at high tides. You will pass a small pond on your right. The foreshore path bears very slightly right. This area is very popular with birdwatchers.

(8) After 400 metres the footpath rejoins the road. This is about half way and a good place to stop for a break, as there are a number of broken slabs of concrete to sit on. Directly in front beyond the mud flats is Gull Island Bird Sanctuary. Follow the road heading NW. The road gradually bears round to the right passing Threestones House.

Beauty in Minature
George Iley CA

Stepping Stones Over
Dark Water
Frank Weller

SouthernMarsh Orchid
Vic Ruston

46

(If the previous section is too difficult, retrace your steps to the alternative footpath mentioned above in **(6)**. Go along this path heading NW for 150 metres. When it meets the road *turn left* and go along the road heading W for 1.2 kms. You will then rejoin the route at the place to stop for a break.)

(9) After 600 metres when the road turns left, join the footpath through a kissing gate in the right-hand corner of the bend. Continue along footpath through the trees. After 200 metres the footpath turns right and goes downhill. Cross a small bridge and continue uphill. The footpath bears slightly left heading NE towards the top left-hand corner of the field.

(10) Cross bridge into field. There is a view of Fawley Power Station Chimney slightly to the left in front. *Turn left* and continue along footpath at edge of field heading NE for 50 metres. *Turn left* to continue along footpath at edge of field heading NW for 300 metres. At bottom of field follow footpath round to the right. Go through gap in hedge and after 50 metres *turn left* through gap in hedge. Continue along left-hand edge of field for 50 metres.

(11) At footpath T-junction *turn right* and continue for 500 metres heading E. Cross road and continue along bridleway for 400 metres heading NE.

(12) After the bridleway bears round to the right, *turn left* along a footpath through a metal gate. Continue along footpath for 400 metres heading NW there is a slight dog-leg to the right about halfway.

(13) At footpath T-junction *turn right.* The footpath then turns left almost immediately and after a few bends you enter a wood. The footpath goes round to the right heading E. After 300 metres you will see a red marker which shows the location of an underground pipeline. Take the left-hand path heading E. After 500 metres of gradually going downhill you will cross a stream by stepping stones. After 50 metres cross or go round a stile and then a small bridge. The footpath then climbs uphill for 100 metres heading NE. Cross stile into field and *turn right* along edge of field for 75 metres, crossing a further stile.

(14) Cross stile at corner of field and *turn left.* Continue along footpath for 50 metres. Cross another stile to join Lepe Road. Whitefield Farm Business Units are immediately in front of you. *Turn right* to return to the start of the walk.

RUTH'S WALK
14. KEYHAVEN AND EFFORD

Walk Length and Time: 10 kms (6 miles) 3½ hours
Starting Point: Main car park in centre of Milford-on-Sea, off
Sea Road, Map Ref: SZ291918

Points of Special Interest
This is one of the few areas where the Forest's historic connection to the Solent
is not cut off by development. The walk also has some glorious sea views, in
particular at (1) when standing on the shingle bank which leads to Hurst Castle and
the lighthouse. To the right (West) you will see Barton, Hengistbury Head, and in
the distance, Poole Bay, Ballard Down (white cliffs) and Anvil Point (Swanage).
Straight ahead (S) are the Needles and the Isle of Wight. To your left is Keyhaven
river behind which is the Solent. Between Hurst Castle and the Isle of Wight is a
fairly narrow waterway (very fast moving tide) which leads into the Solent. Hurst
Castle is one of the many fortifications built along the south coast during the reign
of Henry VIII and extended in the Victorian period.
The area between Milford-on-Sea and Keyhaven will be of great interest to
ornithologists. Keyhaven has hardly changed over the years, so it has retained its
charm. The flood defence wall was designed to resemble a Cornish fishing village.
The river is tidal and practically dries out at low tide except for a narrow channel.
Exceptional high tides can flood the path by the caravan park at the beginning of
the walk, but it is possible to divert around the houses and caravan park and back
onto the path. At **(6)** is a delightful old copse with bluebells in Springtime, a chance
to see deer, but rare to see humans! Also, this very old footpath would have been
well trodden by the villagers of Keyhaven and Milford, when taking their produce
to market or going to church in Lymington.
You may decide to return on a different day and walk along the shingle bank to
Hurst Castle and return by ferry to Keyhaven. Be aware that, if you park your car
on the road at the start of the shingle bank it floods to a depth of 0.5 metres on a
high spring tide. (April and September usually have the highest tides.) At low tide
sea birds invade the mud flats, at high tide windsurfers sometimes take over!

Walking Instructions
✳Start in the far left corner of car park and commence along gravel track, with reed
beds to the right, over a wooden bridge back onto gravel track then onto a quiet
road in a residential area. *Bear right* along road for 90 metres then back onto a
track and continue SE. In the distance you will see the Isle of Wight. Continue for

48

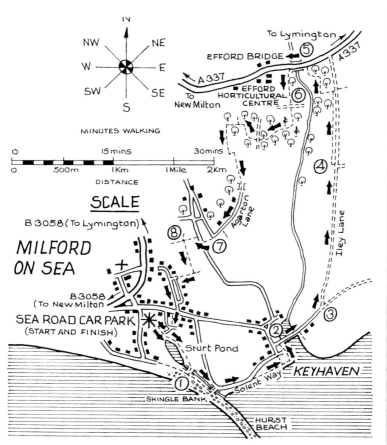

650 metres, with caravan park on left and the tidal river on right to a bridge. Many wading birds can often be seen along here at low tide. Cross over bridge, bear left and follow wide track SE for 150 metres, or scramble up the shingle bank to see marvellous view (see Points of Special Interest).

(1) Continue along shingle bank and, before descending to bridge, read plaque inset in large rock describing sea defences. Cross bridge onto road. Continue E along road with large boulder edging to a 5-bar gate with kissing gate and wheelchair access. Take path along the sea wall to Keyhaven. Pass the jetty, ferry and fishing boats and continue to road in front of Keyhaven Yacht Club. Cross road and take the path to right of Yacht Club along the edge of the harbour with the boat and car park to your left. Public Conveniences are on other side of car park.

(2) On reaching the road, **_turn right_** keeping sea wall and harbour to your right. Ignore footpath sign on right at end of harbour and continue along the road NE marked "No vehicles beyond 200 yards". Continue until you come to a gate across the road, walk round side and in 80 metres **_bear left_** at footpath sign.

(3)   Head N on a well-defined track, Iley Lane, with gorse and blackberry bushes either side; then alongside a landfill site, which is being beautifully returned to nature. Continue for 1¼ kms to minor road.

(4)   Take the *left* path inside the hedge but parallel with the road N for 700 metres, passing through four kissing gates. Climb over the stile and *turn left* W, leaving the minor road. Follow the path around two sides of the field, to another stile, then downhill to a stile onto the road (A337).

(5)   *Turn left* along road for 100 metres crossing Efford Bridge. Just before the bus stop sign on left of road the footpath *turns left* S through a kissing gate into field. Continue S along a well-defined path fenced off from the field and enter a delightful copse via kissing gate.

(6)   After 500 metres the path crosses a track to the Otter Plant Centre on the right. Follow public footpath sign W for 250 metres to three-finger footpath sign. *Turn left* SW and follow path for 600 metres through wood, around field with rows of trees, back into wooded area. The path goes alongside large garden, then onto gravel drive in front of a house at the start of Agarton Lane. (Attractive country properties are on your right.) Continue for 350 metres, ignoring footpath sign opposite thatched house, and take footpath *left* into a field just before right bend in road.

(7)   *Bear right* SW across field to minor road. *Turn right* then almost immediately *left* SW across another field for 250 metres to four-finger footpath sign in middle of field.

(8)   *Turn left* (marked Keyhaven Road) and follow path for 450 metres to T-junction. Keyhaven is straight ahead with the Solent to the left. *Turn right* SW and continue for 200 metres to gate and into residential area. Continue ahead onto road, *turn left* at T-junction and up to main road. *Turn right then almost immediately left*. Cross the road and continue along a green alleyway between the houses. At next road *turn right, then left* into Grebe Close. Follow the road round until you see the path where you started your walk alongside the reed beds. Follow the path back to the car park.

N.B. Towards the end of the walk you pass through large cropped fields. Please respect them and keep any dogs under very close control, preferably on a lead. Do not create a wide trampled path, but just enjoy the lovely views of the Solent and the Isle of Wight.

Fun for all ages - Jim Hotchkiss

Slufters Pool - Robin Fletcher CA

51

Midsummer rain
Christine Thackray

Bridge at Pig Bush - Geoff Betteridge

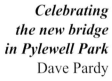

*Celebrating
the new bridge
in Pylewell Park*
Dave Pardy

AUDREY'S WALK
15. ST. LEONARD'S - SOWLEY AND WALHAMPTON

Walk Length and Time: 10 kms (6 miles)   3½ hours

Starting Point: Verge by the large barn, Map Ref: SZ407982

Take the Bucklers Hard road off B3054 SW of Beaulieu village, then bear right at second Y-junction (signposted Sowley). The start is 2 kms (1¼ miles) further on where the road bends sharply right. Park on verge, being careful not to obstruct any entrances.

This linear walk can also be done by taking a train, car or ferry to Lymington Station and then a taxi, or car shuttle with a friend to the start of the walk at St Leonard's Tythe Barn where there is plenty of room to park. You will then walk back to the station.

Points of Special Interest

This walk is part of the Solent Way and, being mainly on quiet country roads, there is no difficulty in route-finding and definitely no hills! The pleasant scenery contrasts wide fields, ancient woods, glimpses of the sea and distant views of the Isle of Wight. St Leonard's where the walk starts, was the site of the chapel dedicated to a French hermit saint who died in 559 AD. The remains of the barn, which was one of the largest in England, indicates the prosperity of Beaulieu Abbey Farms. (For a brilliant short description of Abbey life, read the opening chapters of "The White Company" by Arthur Conan Doyle.) The barn was used for storing fleeces, and the name of nearby Bergerie (French for sheep farm) is significant. There are two interesting diversions off the line of this walk. The first is to Park, previously known as Througham, now thought to be the most likely spot for the murder of King William Rufus, as earliest reports put his death as near a chapel. There was no chapel near the traditional site near Fritham, but there was one at Park, and the name of Througham, when copied and re-copied, may well have been mistakenly written. Less than 120 years after Rufus' death, the Annals of Waverley Abbey in Surrey record "In the year 1204 King John built a Cistercian Abbey which he called Bellus Locus, near the spot where William Rufus was killed."

Park Shore is a beautiful stretch of grassy causeway and beach between pastures, saltmarsh and the Solent, with wonderful views of the Isle of Wight. Although this is a private beach, access permits can be obtained from Beaulieu Estate Office for £1.50 a day, Tel. 01590 612345. Sowley Pond, now a peaceful haven for herons and all sorts of waterfowl once provided the large supply of fish needed for the Abbey. In the 17th and 18th centuries, it was a source of power for the local ironworks, making guns for, amongst others, the East India Company. A nearby house called "Colgrims" is named after the Saxon or Danish owner of the site in the 11th century. As part of a deal to avoid Inheritance Tax, the estate has provided a permissive path along the shore from Tanners Lane to Shotts Lane. At that end, there is a pretty lake and a grassy bank where you could stop for the view and a sandwich. It's your best opportunity to experience undeveloped coastal access in the New Forest. Check the timing of high water and preferably avoid it, but there is also a route a few yards inland if the tide is very high. (See map.) The monument at Walhampton commemorates Admiral Sir Harry Burrard Neale, famous for the refusal of his loyal sailors to join the Nore Mutiny in 1797.

Walking Instructions
Energetic walkers could make the walk circular by using the many other lanes in the area (not many footpaths) and calling for a snack at the East End Arms (see map). Unfortunately there is not currently a right of way along much of the shore. ✳ From the Tythe Barn head broadly W along the lane with its wide grass verges, past Bergerie Farm for about 2 kms.

(1) *Turn left* down Sowley Lane, for another 2½ kms. Shortly after passing Sowley Pond on right, look for a signpost on the right leading into a field. *Turn left* along edge of field for 200 metres and then *turn right* along field edge up to beginning of wood.

(2) *Turn left* and go W through woods and fields to cross road. (At this point turn left and go S down Tanners Lane to use the foreshore alternative.) Continue W and then leave road and use track, past Pylewell Farm.

(3) Go over long footbridge and follow signs past Pylewell House, which is visible on your left. Continue through the park to Shotts Lane where the foreshore path rejoins the route.

(4) *Turn right* N and carry on over crossroads with the ornate gates of Pylewell House on your right.

(5) In 150 metres take gravel track on *left* and continue W past the farm to another lane.

(6) *Turn left* S and in about 100 metres take footpath on *right* opposite wooden house-gates. This is a well-fenced path through woods, leading to a field where you keep the hedge on your right, then cross another track and pass bungalows on the left.

(7) *Turn right* N at the lane and walk about 150 metres to Walhampton Monument with its interesting eulogy to Sir Harry Burrard Neale, where there is verge parking and a bench seat. EITHER retrace your steps back along the lane and continue to main road (300 metres) and turn right (100 metres to Lymington Station and Ferry Terminal); OR turn left W to go beyond Monument and onto path leading to road into Lymington town.

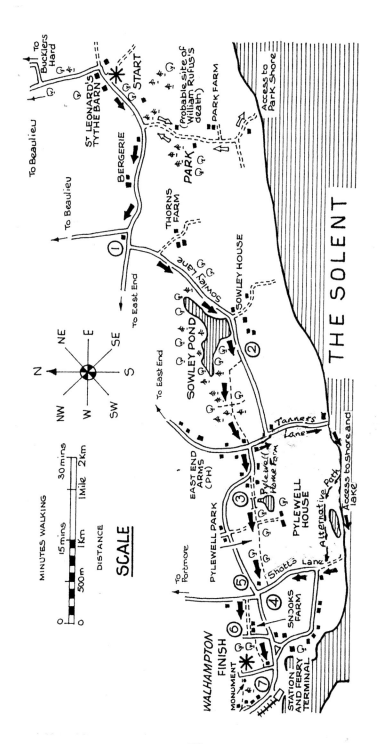

THE SOLENT

Ground Nesting Birds

The New Forest is home to a range of special birds which nest on the ground. They lay their eggs and raise their chicks on the open heathlands and wetlands rather than nesting in trees.

The key nesting season is April, May, June and sometimes into July. So during that period, and especially if you have a dog, stick to tracks and paths and don't allow your dog to go into the undergrowth.

During the nesting season wooded areas are ideal, but even there dogs should always be under control wherever you walk.

Even if you can't see the birds they can see you. Birds such as curlews walk away from their nests temporarily, when disturbed by people, leaving eggs to get cold or vulnerable to predators: so just because you don't see birds taking flight doesn't mean you or your dog are not causing a disturbance.

Ground nesting bird numbers have been decreasing for many reasons, but you **can** make a difference by playing a part in limiting disturbance and giving them the best possible chance of survival.

ACKNOWLEDGMENTS

We are very grateful for the painstaking efforts of the walks' contributors after whom each walk is named, to Marion Cann and Derek Higbee for the original word processing and compilation and to Jack Street for drawing the maps and, last but not least, to the dozen ramblers who have helped in keeping this book fully up-to-date.

The photographs marked CA are the copyright of the Countryside Agency, a predecessor of Natural England.